PHOTOGRAPH: LOU HANSEN

Peter McConchie has worked internationally as a professional photographer for over ten years, specialising in fashion and portraiture. Since returning to Australia in 1997 he has travelled the country, following his love of the ocean and dedicating himself to environmental projects and recording Aboriginal stories.

AUSTRALIA

BEYOND ANY PRICE

photography and text by **PETER McCONCHIE**

MACMILLAN

Pan Macmillan Australia

TO BELINDA BARDAS AND LOU HANSEN, THANK YOU FOR YOUR DEDICATION AND SUPPORT IN THE MAKING OF *AUSTRALIA: BEYOND ANY PRICE*. AND THANK YOU TO IAN RICHARDSON FOR HIS TIRELESS ROLE IN HELPING TO CREATE THIS BOOK.

First published 2001 in Macmillan by Pan Macmillan Australia Pty Limited
St Martins Tower, 31 Market Street, Sydney
Text and photographs copyright © Peter McConchie 2001
Contributing photography (Great Barrier Reef) copyright © Michael Collins and Nick Tonks 2001

National Library of Australia
Cataloguing-in-Publication data:

McConchie, Peter
Australia: Beyond any price

ISBN 0 7329 1102 8

1. Landscape – Australia – Pictorial works. 2. Wilderness areas –
Australia – Pictorial works. 3. Nature conservation – Australia.
4. Environmental protection – Australia. 5. Australia – Pictorial works.
6. Australia – Description and travel. I. Title.

919.400222

Cover and text designed by Liz Seymour, Seymour Designs
Printed by Markono Print Media Pte Ltd

Photograph on page 2: The Great Victoria Desert, South Australia.
Photograph on page 6: A waterhole at Kakadu in the Northern Territory.

FOREWORD Australians are a diverse people, but if we share one value, it is a common love of our unique natural environment.

This collection of breathtaking images captures the true spirit of our Australian landscape. Through Peter's loving eye, we witness what remains of our pristine wilderness areas. These pictures celebrate the unforgettable beauty of our great land, but also serve as a reminder of what we have lost, and what our children stand to lose if we fail to acknowledge our responsibilities.

I sincerely hope that future generations of Australians are left with more than these beautiful images and sorry excuses. I am honoured to be involved in such a worthwhile and important project, and hope you enjoy this book as much as I have.

JANET HOLMES À COURT

CONTENTS

Supporters

This book was created with the help of many individuals and organisations. Their willingness to become involved in *Australia: Beyond Any Price* demonstrates to Government and Industry that community support for our environment cannot be ignored.

WITH SINCERE THANKS TO

Peter Alexander, Tina Arena, Peter Avery, Maria Babalouka, Sandra and David Bardas, John Bennetts, Daniel Besen, Natalie Bloom, Bev and Peter Brock, Graeme and Renee Brown, Sally Browne, Nellie Castan, Liz Davenport, Tottie Goldsmith, Rebecca Hetrel, Claire Konkes, Jack Lim, Peggy McConchie, Jo McKeena, Jenny Munster, Grant and Stuart Nicol, Steve Renolds, Jill Riechstein, Vicki Vidor, Heloise Waislitz and Graeme Wise.

American Re-Insurance Company, Bakpakka, Blakes Restaurant, Bogong Equipment, Bond Imaging Pty Ltd, Chadwick Management, The Church St Pantry, Connecting Images, Elsternwick Primary School, FDR Business Services, Margaret Porritt (Feathers), Ford, Fuji Film, General Pants, Gloweave, Lab X, Linfox Property Group, Melbourne Complementary Medicine, Melrose Health Supplies, Metalicus, Mikoshi, Mooroolbark Technologies Pty Ltd, Noodle Box, The Planet Earth Cleaning Company, Seven, Spiral Foods, Split Rock, The Stock Liquidator, St John's Ambulance, TAG Heuer, Roy, Room Interior Products, Werribee Optus and explus.

Forest light.

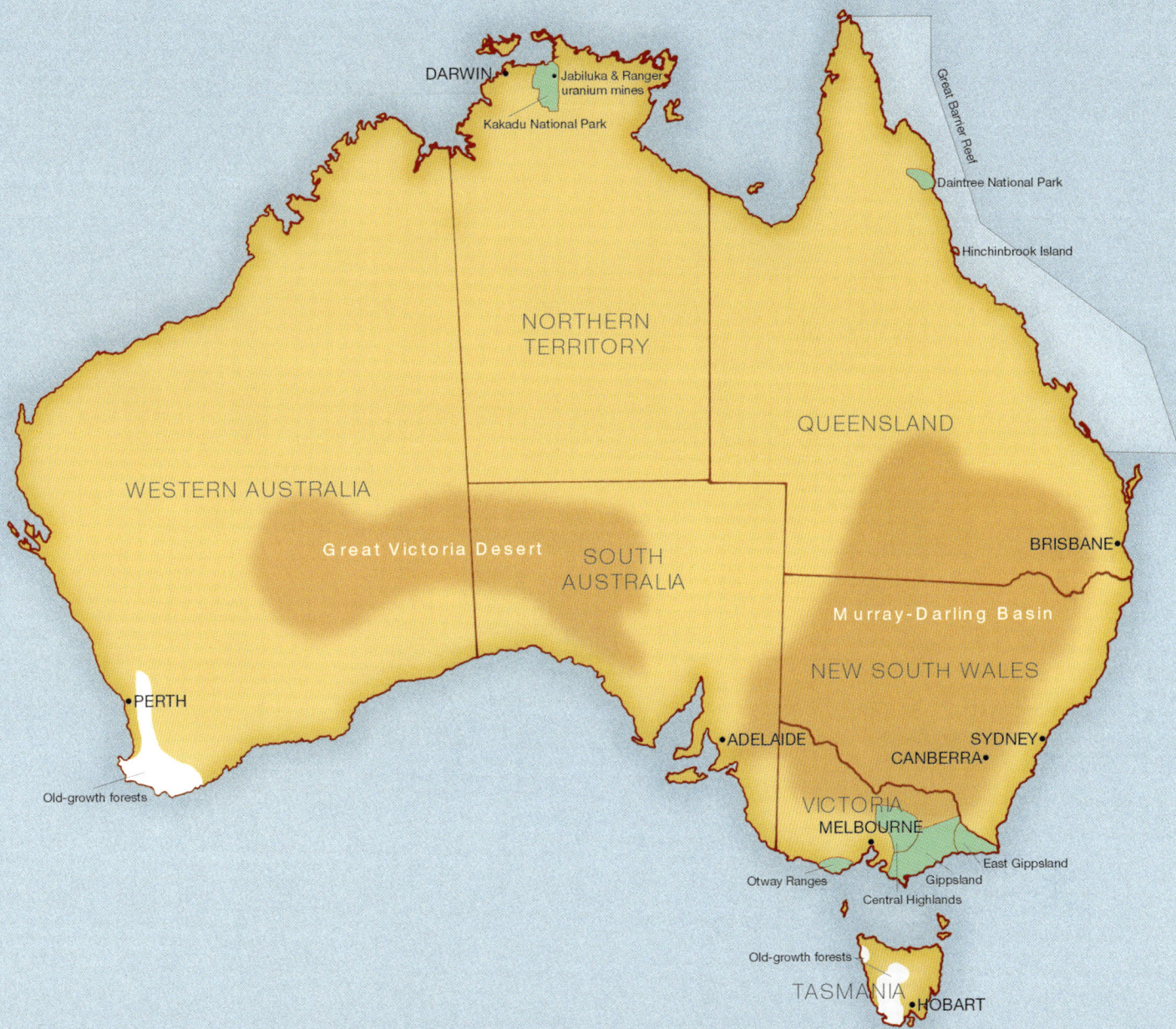

DARWIN

Jabiluka & Ranger
uranium mines

Kakadu National Park

Great Barrier Reef

Daintree National Park

Hinchinbrook Island

NORTHERN
TERRITORY

QUEENSLAND

WESTERN AUSTRALIA

Great Victoria Desert

SOUTH
AUSTRALIA

BRISBANE

Murray-Darling Basin

NEW SOUTH WALES

PERTH

Old-growth forests

ADELAIDE

SYDNEY
CANBERRA

VICTORIA
MELBOURNE

East Gippsland

Otway Ranges

Gippsland

Central Highlands

Old-growth forests

TASMANIA

HOBART

INTRODUCTION

Most of my working life has been spent as a fashion and portrait photographer, which has taken me to such cities as New York, London, Paris and Milan. Photography has been good to me, but increasingly I found it hard to combine my career in fashion with a growing desire to follow my interest in the important issues of our times, such as the environment and reconciliation. This book is the story of my journey away from cities and towards a reconnection with the land.

After spending many years travelling and working overseas, I came back to Australia in 1997. Not long after returning, I visited a little-known place called Goolengook Forest in East Gippsland, Victoria. At that time Goolengook was being clear-felled and the forest's enormous trees were being turned into woodchips to make paper products. I was deeply concerned that a two-million-year-old ecosystem was being threatened by a logging company for the sake of cheap trees. Frustrated about this destruction, I produced a calendar to raise awareness and funds for the environmental groups that were defending the ancient forest.

Following my experiences in Goolengook, I decided to create a book that would make environmental issues more understandable and more accessible for people outside the green movement. The book began as a photographic study of Australia's remaining pristine wild lands. My aim was to remind people that these places are internationally recognised as some of the most important and diverse ecosystems on earth. I also wanted to provide information about the threats posed to these environments by inappropriate forms of development.

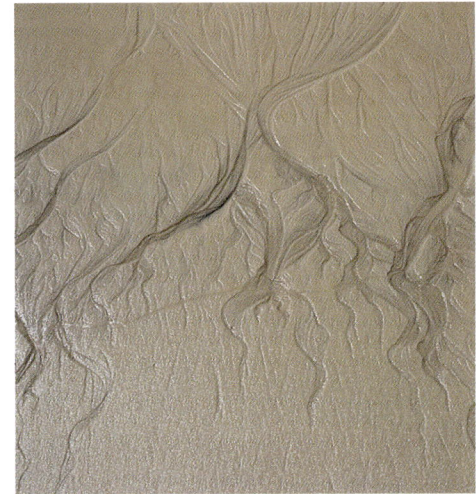

ABOVE Hinchinbrook Island.
OPPOSITE 'Dolphin', Goolengook Forest, East Gippsland.

'Dog rock', Victoria.

Starting out with a working title and a basic proposal I approached TAG Heuer Watches, the client I was shooting for at the time, to ask how I should go about getting support. TAG, along with the Ford Motor Company, came on board early as key supporters and gave me advice on how to involve people and organisations in the project. Most importantly, their willingness to back the idea and lend their names to the book gave me the resolve and determination I needed to take the first steps towards making it happen.

To produce a book that would cover much of Australia and highlight the threats faced by environments such as forests, desert country and the sea, I decided to travel to every state and the Northern Territory. Within each state I focused on areas of international significance, where unique and fragile environments are under threat of destruction as a result of weak laws and outdated commercial activities. Rather than photograph the shocking images of salt-ravaged paddocks and exhausted waterways, I focused on places of immense beauty.

The photography was undertaken between June 1998 and February 1999, as I travelled anticlockwise around Australia, visiting Victoria, New South Wales, Queensland, the Northern Territory, Western Australia, South Australia and Tasmania. I began the trip in Victoria with two companions, Lou Hansen, who worked as my photographic assistant, and Matthew Mackay, who did the cooking while he travelled with us as far as Sydney. Once I had decided on a subject — such as a riverbank or a stand of trees — we spent four or five days in the area watching the variations in the light and weather conditions, and exploring, looking for information and more places to photograph. With the budget running low, Lou returned home after the Daintree. From there I travelled alone from the Queensland coast to Kakadu National Park in the Northern Territory.

Where possible, I made contact with local people who were involved in ongoing environmental campaigns. In the Great Victoria Desert in South Australia I met the Kupa Piti Kungka Tjutia, also known as the Kungkas. The Kungkas are senior women elders from a number of communities who live on traditional lands in the desert. They lived through the time of the British nuclear tests at Maralinga and Emu Junction in the 1950s. Today the women are fighting to prevent the construction of a nuclear waste dump on or near their land. The locations that are being considered would place the dump site dangerously close to the Great Artesian Basin, one of the largest underground reservoirs of fresh water on earth.

During the three weeks I spent with the Kungkas at Ten Mile Creek I took photos for them to use in their efforts to get press coverage for the campaign. Although it was often tempting to do so, this was the only time I stopped working on the book and became involved in one of the issues it covers.

After the photography came the text. In February 2000 I began to compile resources on each of the areas covered in the book and to contact universities, individual scientists, traditional owners and other experts who are leaders in their fields. As you will see from the list of Chapter Editors, I have had the assistance of many eminent Australians, who gave their time and expertise to read the chapters and to ensure the accuracy of the information contained in them.

Australia: Beyond Any Price took eighteen months to bring together and was only possible with the help of the book's supporters, who were willing to do something to highlight our country's natural treasures and their importance to our survival.

Across the Australian community a general consensus is forming that we do care about protecting our environment. We understand that this means halting development in some areas and rejecting many long-held ideas. People like me, and like the supporters listed in this book, are not necessarily greenies, academics or politicians. We want effective laws that protect the environment and its biodiversity from further degradation or loss. We recognise the need for industry and individuals to preserve the environment and act responsibly for future generations.

PETER McCONCHIE

Morning leaves.

LAND AND WATER

THE MURRAY-DARLING BASIN

ABOVE Kangaroo skeleton in the Murray-Darling Basin.
PREVIOUS PAGE: Murray River, Victoria–New South
Wales border.
OPPOSITE River gum growing by the Darling River,
New South Wales.

The Murray-Darling Basin, extending from the Australian alps to the semi-arid plains of the Darling River, contains an enormous variety of landscapes and environments. Covering a million square kilometres, about one-seventh of the Australian continent, it takes in over 75 per cent of New South Wales, over 50 per cent of Victoria, 15 per cent of Queensland and 7 per cent of South Australia. Two million people live within the Basin area. More than twenty major rivers flow through it, rushing down narrow winding gullies from the Great Dividing Range, spreading across the huge inland flood plains, and spilling into the Southern Ocean.

Approximately 40 per cent of Australia's agricultural production is derived from industries based in the area. It supports three-quarters of Australia's irrigated farmland, producing 90 per cent of our irrigated field crops, 80 per cent of our pasture and lucerne, 70 per cent of our fruit crops and 25 per cent of our vegetables. Wool and dairy goods are produced in the region, and cattle and sheep are also farmed there for the domestic and overseas markets.

Now this enormous part of Australia is in crisis. The diversity and abundance of native fish, mammals, birds, reptiles and invertebrates are being seriously affected by changes to rivers, wetlands, flood plains, billabongs, and riparian vegetation. Past and ongoing clearing practices, as well as pollution from agriculture and sewage, represent the biggest threat to the indigenous plants and animals of the Murray-Darling Basin. Loss of bushland leads to serious salinity and erosion problems and, combined with the degraded state of the remaining areas of bushland, means there is insufficient habitat to ensure the survival of many species.

Salinity, or a concentration of salt in the soil, is caused by the clearing of deep-rooted vegetation to make way for shallow-rooted annual crops and pastures. This results in a significant reduction in water use and thus, rising watertables. Once the watertable is consistently within 1 metre of the surface, the salts that exist naturally in the soil are carried to the surface with the water. When these salts have risen, they can enter the rivers and kill the remaining vegetation. It is expected that nearly all irrigation regions within the Basin will have watertables within 2 metres of the surface by 2010.

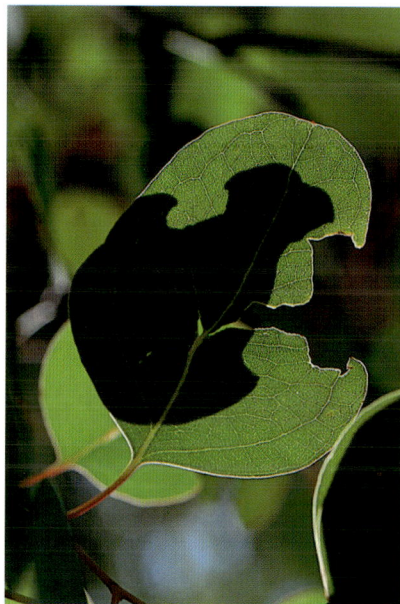

LEFT Native pine.
RIGHT Gum leaf.
OPPOSITE 'Frog and koala' rocks,
New South Wales.

Salinity is not only a problem in irrigated areas. It is now recognised that dry-land salinisation, brought on by changes to vegetation cover and agriculture, has the potential to affect an even greater area and contribute further to rising salt levels in our rivers. If current trends continue, within twenty years the water drawn from the Murray River to supply Adelaide's tap water could be too salty to drink on an average of two days out of every five.

The impact of irrigation infrastructure for agriculture – dams, weirs and flow regulation – together with the high demand for water resources are also prime contributors to the decline in ecological functioning in the Murray-Darling river system. The storage and supply of water for irrigated agriculture have reduced the natural flow to the sea by more than 80 per cent. Salinisation and waterlogging have been caused by the removal of vegetation for irrigation. If the rivers and wetlands of the Murray-Darling Basin are to survive they need environmental flows. This means

ABOVE Young gum blossoms, New South Wales.
OPPOSITE The mallee.

'Rock chief'.

using less water for irrigated agriculture. We must also remove many of the unnecessary barriers to fish passage, such as weirs and barrages, and install fish ladders in those that remain.

Conventional farming practices and the poor management of agricultural land create and increase the problems in the Basin area. Repeated applications of ammonia-based fertilisers, for example, can contribute to soil acidification by changing the chemistry of the soil. It often takes many years for plant yields to decline, so farmers have only recently begun to realise that their land-management practices are resulting in acidic soils. Also, agriculture contributes significantly to the large amounts of sediments being carried into the rivers. Nutrients found in the soil are washed away from the land, where they are needed for plant growth, and into the waterways, lowering the soil nutrient level and polluting the water. To limit erosion and the movement of sediment to the rivers it is important to maintain a vegetative cover, particularly on land along stream and river frontages, to act as a filter and to keep livestock away from riverbanks.

As well as washing nutrients from the soil into the river, irrigation drainage and urban sewage represent significant sources of pollutants and microbiological and bacterial contamination

'Bark man dreaming'.

ABOVE Afternoon delight.
OPPOSITE Barmah Forest, alongside
the Murray River.

such as E. coli and giardia. Toxic blooms of blue–green algae also constitute a complex problem. A healthy river system generally has many types of plants and animals that make use of naturally occurring algae. However, when the natural checks and balances present in the river system change, toxic blooms can grow. This growth is assisted by changes such as the diversion of water for irrigation, the proliferation of locks and weirs, and decreased natural river flows and high nutrient levels, especially phosphorus. Given these conditions, some species of blue–green algae form poisonous blooms which choke the life out of the water.

For the most part, the solutions to these problems, especially salinity, require changes to vegetation cover right across the Murray-Darling landscape. Revegetation, plantations and changed agricultural practices involving 'salt friendly' cropping and grazing systems are the major weapons in the war against salt. We can begin by retaining and protecting all the native vegetation cover in the region and by encouraging natural regeneration of indigenous vegetation, for example, by fencing-off land which can re-seed from remnant trees and from adjacent vegetated areas.

What is needed most is a dedicated, co-operative effort from the four Murray-Darling Basin states to repair and reverse the ongoing degradation.

FORESTS

TASMANIA

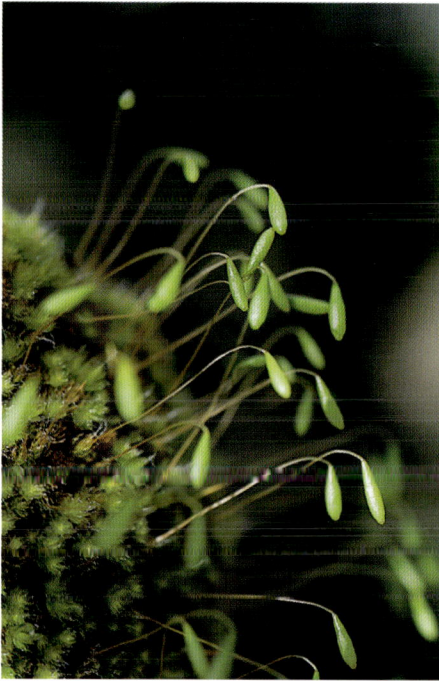

ABOVE Micro forest.
PREVIOUS PAGE 'The magic forest', Tasmania.
OPPOSITE Lorinna, Tasmania.

Tasmania's eucalypt forests are among the most spectacular in the world, and are home to an enormous diversity of wildlife including wedge-tailed eagles, pygmy possums, white goshawks, black cockatoos and owls. The island state has the tallest hardwood trees on the planet, as well as the world's tallest flowering plant, the swamp gum. In the north-west you find Australia's largest tract of temperate rainforest. Tasmania's rainforests include stands of Huon pine — closely related to a species found in New Zealand — individual trees of which can live for more than 3000 years. The Tasmanian rainforests are relics of the ancient supercontinent of Gondwana, which included what is now Australia, New Zealand, India, Antarctica and parts of Africa and South America.

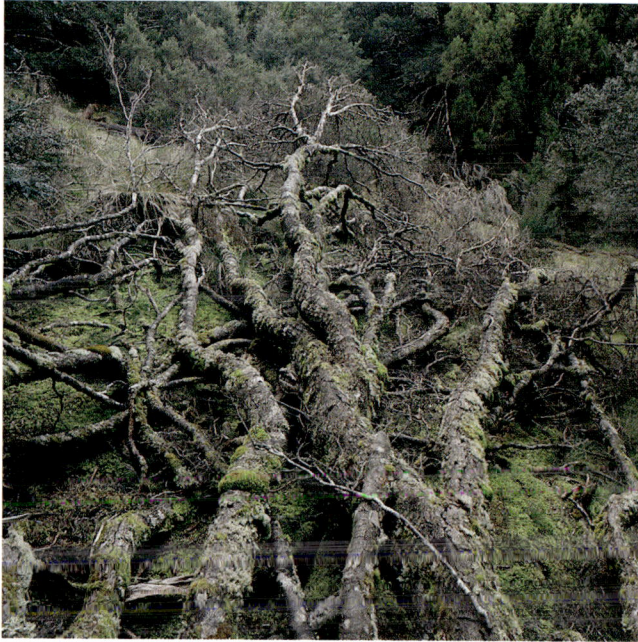

As this book went to press, less than 13 per cent of the original eucalypt forest was left, and the remnants are being logged at a horrific rate to be used as furniture veneer, sawlogs and pulp. The felling of trees continues to escalate with new roads being cut into pristine old-growth areas. Some of the species being logged are myrtle, sassafras, stringybark, swamp gum, gum-topped stringybark and celery top pine. Many of Tasmania's towering forests lie in deep valleys adjoining World Heritage Areas. Their conservation values have been confirmed by experts in World Heritage assessments, yet over 40,000 hectares of unprotected old-growth forest remain open to logging.

LEFT Clearly felled.
OPPOSITE 'Sacred water'.

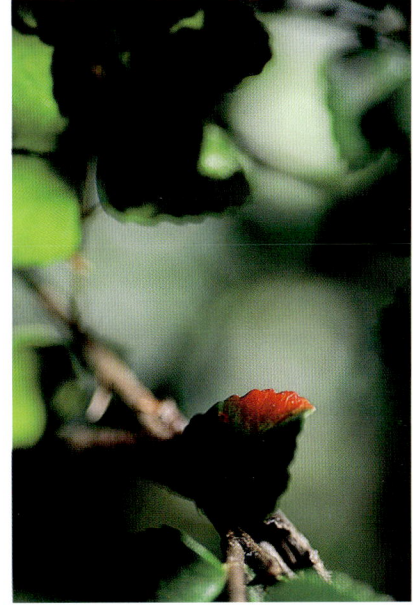

ABOVE 'Tiny fingers'.
CENTRE 'Fighting fern'.
RIGHT A touch of red.
OPPOSITE 'Emu crossing'.

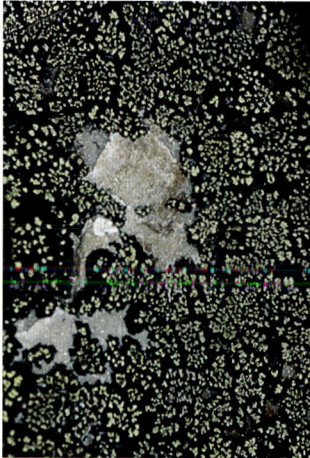

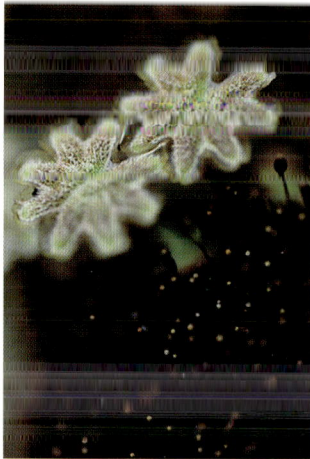

TOP Casper moss.
ABOVE Forest stars.
OPPOSITE The mossy five.

Several companies are making large amounts of money from chipping Tasmanian and mainland native forest. These forests were not planted by the companies logging them. They have been growing for at least 10,000 years. Government subsidies for the logging industry help to maintain the profitability of harvesting old-growth forests. Without this financial support – courtesy of the taxpayer – the economics of logging these trees would be dramatically altered in favour of plantation timbers. Current laws allow for unlimited export of woodchips from old growth in state forests and private land in Tasmania.

This destruction does not only affect the trees. Carrot bait, impregnated with 1080 poison to kill wallabies and possums that eat pasture or plantation seedlings, is laid in Tasmanian forests each year by organisations connected to the logging industry. The amount laid is enough to kill about half a million native animals across many different species. Safe, inexpensive alternatives for protecting crops from these animals, such as fences and tree guards, are widely available.

The companies involved in logging native forests are not immune to action from concerned individuals. A boycott of Canadian logging giant MacMillan Bloedel affected sales so much that the company agreed to end the destructive practice of clear-felling native forests in Canada. This is an indication of the strength of public awareness and of organised campaigning. Many Tasmanians are presently fighting the logging of old-growth forests and are involved in the massive conversion of native forests to plantations taking place in the state. Supporters from the rest of Australia and the rest of the world are needed to help defend what remains of the ancient forests of Tasmania.

Chapter Editor: Professor Jamie Kirkpatrick

WESTERN AUSTRALIA

ABOVE Walpole bloom.
OPPOSITE Old-growth karri, Western Australia.
FOLLOWING PAGE Burnt but alive.

The forests of Western Australia's south-west are perched precariously on a corner of this otherwise arid part of the continent. They grow within about 100 kilometres of the coast and stretch from just north of Perth to east of Albany in the south. The dominant trees are familiar names to a Western Australian: jarrah, marri, karri and blackbutt, tingle and tuart. While the main tree species are the same across the forested range, and the forests might appear superficially similar, the diversity of plant and animal life within them is extraordinary. This part of the continent is unique, as are the plants and animals found there, since they have been isolated from their nearest relatives in south-eastern Australia for millions of years.

Old-growth forests include a mix of ancient and sometimes extremely large trees and new trees of varying sizes. They have rich soil, broad canopies and deep leaf litter. Rotting logs in the forests hold moisture all year round and provide a habitat for rare flora and fauna. Logging and frequent burning to increase timber values dry out the forests and destroy critical ecosystems. Jarrah, marri and karri are the trees most sought after by logging operators in Western Australia. Cutting them for timber over many years and more recently the intensified logging for woodchipping have depleted these forests drastically.

How much old-growth forest is left? The estimate depends on what you define as 'old growth'. Of the more common forest types, such as karri, about one-third still exists. The statistics for the once expansive jarrah forests are not so good: only around 2 per cent of old growth remains.

ABOVE Sunshine within.
PREVIOUS PAGE Walpole,
Western Australia.
OPPOSITE Frankland River, Walpole.

ABOVE 'Delight'.
RIGHT 'Breeze'.
OPPOSITE Old growth, Walpole.

The more we log our forests, the drier and the more prone to fire our land becomes. As we have fewer forests to hold moisture, we may get less rain and the forests may retract even further. As they diminish in size, the more prone they are to disease and to invasion from weeds and feral animals.

Many people of Western Australia have long realised, and many more are beginning to recognise, the need to preserve these majestic forests. Conservationists have been joined by scientists, doctors, businesspeople, sporting identities and people from all walks of life and political persuasions in a campaign to save what remains. Their work to raise public awareness has led to a government promise to protect the remaining old-growth forest in south-western Australia.

Chapter Editor: Dr Pierre Horwitz

TOP 'Croc jaw'.
LEFT 'Pixi'.
OPPOSITE 'Old man', Walpole.

VICTORIA

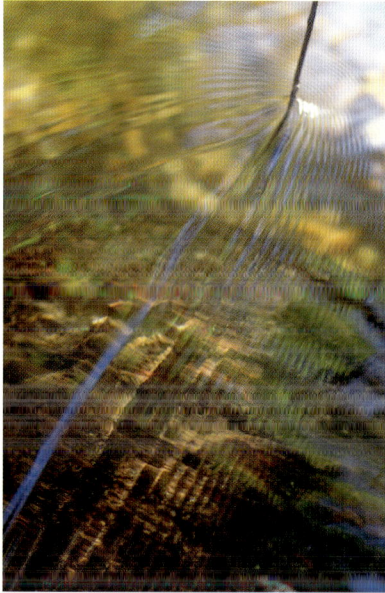

ABOVE River at Goolengook.
OPPOSITE Triplet Falls, the Otways.

East Gippsland extends from Lakes Entrance along the Victorian coast to the New South Wales border, and north to the Great Dividing Range. Spanning from the coast to the alps, the forests of this area are recognised for their World Heritage value, supporting over 300 rare and threatened species of plant life. They also provide the remaining stronghold for a number of endangered animals including the long-footed potoroo, the tiger quoll, the sooty owl and the Orbost spiny crayfish, all of which depend on East Gippsland's trees and pristine water catchments for their survival.

Australia has been separated from the supercontinent of Gondwana for 65 million years. Over the last two million years it has been exposed to nineteen ice ages, the last ending about 10,000 years ago. During that time its ecosystems have been constantly adapting and changing; East Gippsland is a wonderful example of this evolution.

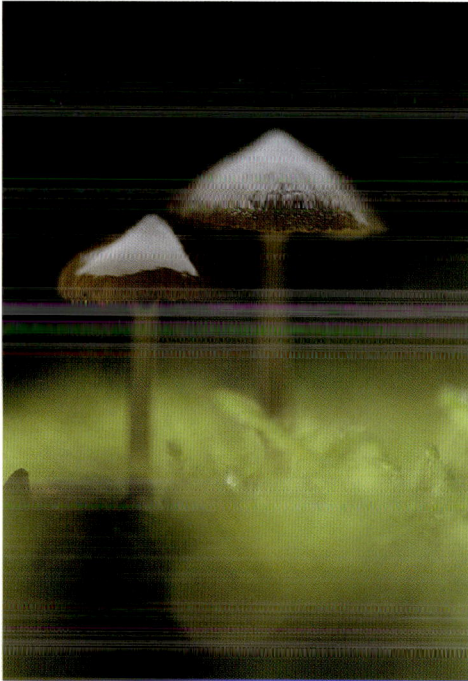

ABOVE AND OPPOSITE New and old growth in
the Otway Ranges.

In one logging season, which lasts approximately six months, about 200 coupes in East Gippsland are scheduled for clear-felling. At its largest, a logging coupe is approximately the size of 400 urban house blocks, or 40 hectares. However, many are smaller. After clear-felling, these areas are planted with commercially desirable species, destroying the natural diversity which existed within the old forests.

Taxpayers' money is used to finance the clear felling – or large-scale destruction – of Victoria's forests. Unfortunately, state government subsidies create an incentive for accelerated logging from old-growth areas, as the trees are cheaper than plantation timber. This is despite the fact that Victoria already has enough plantations ready for harvesting to supply all our timber and paper needs. This would create 2000 jobs in the process. It seems a waste to prop up an ailing industry that not only costs the government, but which has a negative impact on adjacent industries such as tourism, agriculture and manufacturing.

The green movement has made some progress in defending these forests. Under the Regional Forest Agreement, which was signed in 1997, nearly half the region's 1.2 million hectares was protected from logging. However, the agreement only goes so far. There is no limit to the volume of woodchips that can be exported from the areas still open to logging.

The forests of Goolengook are one part of East Gippsland that has been preserved until recent years. The area has three types of Victorian rainforest: cool temperate, warm temperate and warm–cool overlap. In 1998, the Victorian Government's scientists described the Goolengook area as the best opportunity in the state for these classes of rainforest to be preserved. Despite this recommendation, logging in the region commenced on 5 June 1998, the eve of World Environment Day.

ABOVE Old-growth forest, Apollo Bay.
OPPOSITE 'Going up'.

Another area of Victoria being degraded by logging is the Central Highlands. Covering over one million hectares to the north-east of Melbourne, the Highlands are renowned for their beauty and the diverse range of fauna and flora that can be found in their reserves and state forests. Stands of mountain ash on the higher slopes form the defining image of the area, while drier forests of messmate, peppermint and stringybark cover the lower slopes. The Central Highlands are vital to Victoria's tourism industry and to the state's water supply. The area attracts around 850,000 visitors each year. Most of Melbourne's water catchments are found here, providing a source of domestic drinking water to over three million people within and around the city. But logging continues in this region and affects both the water quality and supply. An old-growth forest yields almost twice the water of a forest that is clear-felled every 40 to 80 years. Destroying the water catchments and surrounding forests ultimately results in increased risk of landslides, soil erosion and mud-choked water.

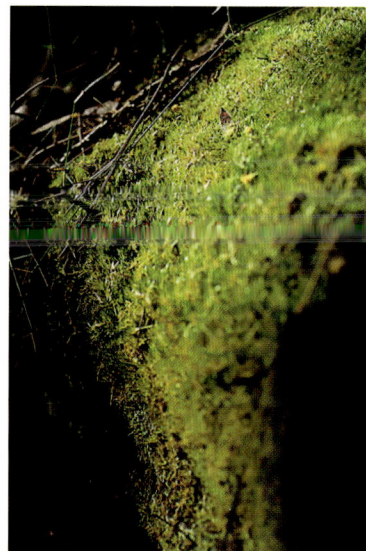

ABOVE RIGHT Central Highlands spirit.
BELOW RIGHT Mossy log.
OPPOSITE Apollo Bay old growth.

A further consequence of logging in the Central Highlands is the destruction of the habitats of rare native fauna. After a 250-year-old tree is felled, the surrounding forest continues to be logged in 60- to 80-year rotations. As a result, diverse ecosystems supporting animals dependant on tree hollows, which exist only in an old-growth forest, are not given the chance to grow back.

At the time of this book's publication there was extensive logging and woodchipping in the Otway Ranges to the west of Melbourne. The Otway forests provide drinking water to over 250,000 people in western Victoria, yet half of the logging in the region occurs in the water catchment areas. The economic future of the Otways rests on a growing tourist industry worth over $300 million annually. This industry depends on the maintenance of the region's assets, which includes the forests now under threat from logging and woodchipping.

Our native forests and water catchments are being clear-felled to make paper products. In a few years it may be the case that the only old-growth forests still standing are those protected in national parks.

Chapter Editor: Dr Barry Traill

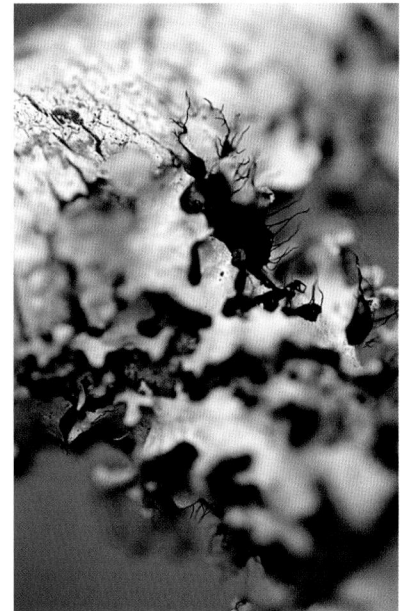

ABOVE 'Black bunny', the Otways.
OPPOSITE Goolengook Forest.

URBANISATION

THE DAINTREE, QUEENSLAND

LEFT New.
RIGHT Old.
OPPOSITE Host and strangler.
PREVIOUS PAGE Cape Tribulation, Queensland.

The Daintree in North Queensland extends some 70 kilometres north of the Daintree River to the Bloomfield River. Much of the rainforest in this area grows on the steep mountain slopes of the coastal range, which rises to over 1000 metres. However, what most people refer to as the 'Daintree' are the coastal lowlands between the Daintree River and Cape Tribulation – between the mountains and the sea. This area contains the only remaining example of tropical lowland forests still intact and still connected to both upland forests and forests that fringe the sea.

The area is regarded by biologists as a living museum of plant species, many of which originated millions of years ago on the Gondwana supercontinent. Covering approximately 20,000 hectares, the coastal lowlands have probably the highest diversity of plant families found anywhere in the world. Over 2500 species

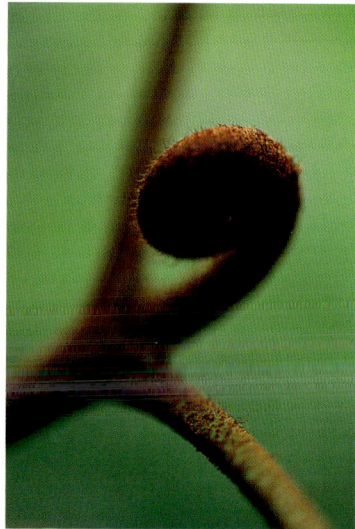

TOP Cape Tribulation.
ABOVE AND OPPOSITE The
Daintree.

of flowering plants grow in these tropical forests, including a diverse range of limited endemic species, that is, plants that are found nowhere else on earth. The natural habitat of some of these plants is restricted to an area smaller than a football field.

Within and around the Daintree's plant life, rare animals such as Bennett's tree kangaroo and the diurnal rat kangaroo make their home. Many animals and birds have evolved together in such intricate ways that they need certain plants for food and shelter. Trees often require bats and birds for pollination and dispersion of their seeds. The cassowary eats the fallen fruit of over 70 different species of plants and deposits the seeds, together with fertiliser, elsewhere in the forest.

Despite their remoteness, the Daintree lowlands are under threat. Surprisingly, pressure from tourism is not the main concern; in fact tourists are responsible for relatively little actual degradation and damage to the forests. The most significant threat comes from settlement and urbanisation. In the late 1970s, a total of 1127 freehold allotments were created in the lowland Daintree and offered for public sale. Most of these blocks were sold and there are now about 200 permanent households in the area. The remainder of the purchased blocks are currently unoccupied, but are open for development at any time. With freehold land comes an 'as of right' permission to clear land for house sites and access.

The Daintree was the subject of an international outcry over the construction of the Bloomfield Track between Cape Tribulation and the Bloomfield River in 1984. The importance of the region and its plants and animals was formally recognised in 1988 when 900,000 hectares of tropical habitat between Townsville and Cooktown were declared a Wet Tropics World Heritage Area. National parks and state forests are covered by World Heritage protection, but most of the privately owned subdivided lowland rainforest remains at risk from urbanisation.

Despite, and perhaps because of, World Heritage listing, settlement continues today, and with increasing numbers of settlers comes growing pressure for infrastructure, particularly grid power. Provision of electricity to the area has been a major political issue. The current Queensland Government has partially addressed the problem by installing renewable power systems in the area, making it (with over 150 installed systems) one of the largest renewable power communities in the world. However, many settlers feel that renewable energy systems are not an adequate substitute for grid power connection. In an area that has humidity levels of up to 95 per cent, provision of grid electricity would allow the installation of air conditioning. This would greatly accelerate the rate of settlement. With this settlement will come increasing demands for schools, shops, hospitals and a bridge across the Daintree River. With that, any hopes of sustaining these rainforests into the future are seriously threatened.

ABOVE Buttress, Daintree.
OPPOSITE Mossman, North Queensland.

Increased settlement can only endanger the biological integrity of the region. Of the 120 known rare and threatened plant species in the Daintree lowlands, 85 are found on unprotected private land and some are only found on freehold blocks. One tree, a member of the mahogany family, appears to have become extinct through the clearing of land. The Daintree is also experiencing a massive invasion of introduced plants. The Singapore Daisy is the most noticeable, although members of the arum-lily family are also growing prolifically. In the absence of their natural predators, these imported tropical species are rapidly growing out of control. Coconuts are threatening to replace the rainforest trees growing near many of the Daintree's most isolated beaches. Scientists also think that human impact is responsible for the loss of a number of once common frog species found in the region.

In 1994, the Queensland Labor Government, in co-operation with the Federal Government of the day, funded a $23 million Daintree Rescue Package. Half of the money was used to buy back important blocks of land, and the other half for visitor infrastructure. Buy-back, whether through private or government funding, has always been the most politically acceptable way of ensuring the Daintree's future biological integrity. Land prices were not keeping pace with inflation, and most absentee land owners were keen to sell, in fact, the original Daintree buy-back announcement was greeted with over 500 offers of Daintree land. However, the buy-back of freehold blocks has always been perceived as a politically sensitive issue and implementation depends on the attitude of the current government. Conservation groups can only raise limited funds to buy back land themselves. Thus the future of the Daintree rests in the hands of politicians who will only respond to increasing pressure from the public.

Chapter Editor: Dr Hugh Spencer

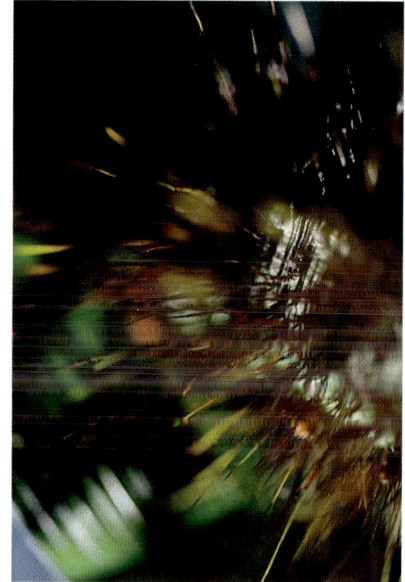

ABOVE Morning fern.
OPPOSITE Mossman Gorge.

PRECIOUS RESOURCES

THE GREAT BARRIER REEF, QUEENSLAND

The Great Barrier Reef extends from just north of Fraser Island to the tip of Cape York, and covers 351,400 square kilometres, equivalent to the size of Italy. By far the largest single collection of coral reefs in the world, the Reef supports one of the earth's most beautiful and biologically diverse ecosystems.

The marine park contains around 4,700 coastal and off-shore coral reefs, sand keys and islands. In the inter-reef, which makes up 25 per cent of the area, there are gardens of sea fans, sponges and deep algal mounds. A variety of animals dwell in the soft sand and mud, and on rocky outcrops and submerged ancient reefs. The inner-lagoon, which covers around 33 per cent of the Reef, consists of sandy and muddy sea floor interspersed with coral outcrops. This is the habitat of many types of starfish, shellfish and sponge, and is teeming with fish and prawns.

A recent study identified 765 species of sea-floor organisms in just one area of the Great Barrier Reef. Few of these species have been studied scientifically and many are not even named. The continental slope on the outer edge plunges from a water depth of about 80 to 800 metres. Representing about 36 per cent of the World Heritage Area, this section is almost completely unexplored. It is thought to house a range of slow-growing organisms which have been undisturbed for thousands of years.

The Great Barrier Reef is the largest of the world's 552 World Heritage Areas, joining the ranks of these Heritage Areas in 1981. World Heritage status means that a country accepts an obligation to do all it can to identify, protect and conserve the natural and cultural heritage of the area for future generations. The Great Barrier Reef Marine Park, which is considered the best-protected reef system worldwide, is managed with a goal of maintaining its ecological qualities while allowing sustainable uses from tourism, fishing and shipping, and all use is regulated by a permit system. However, for its first twenty years as a World Heritage Area, less than 5 per cent of the Reef was no-take zones. In recent years there has been a growing realisation of the need to identify and protect a larger and more representative cross-section of the Reef, and fortunately zoning systems are now being revised.

A wide range of fishing industries operate in Great Barrier Reef waters, with prawn trawlers and commercial and recreational line and net fishers being the most important users. Commercial trawling is considered the most destructive, and at present levels unsustainable,

LEFT 'A hidden face', Great Barrier Reef. PHOTOGRAPH: MICHAEL COLLINS

activity in the Great Barrier Reef. Trawlers drag a heavy chain across the sea floor, which dislodges and crushes all but the toughest organisms in its path. A single pass of a trawl net can remove 5 to 25 per cent of bottom-dwelling organisms, including large sponges and flower pot corals, and thirteen passes can kill off up to 70 to 90 per cent of sea-floor organisms. Trawling results in the capture of a far greater range of species than those targeted, including large creatures such as sea snakes and marine turtles. It is estimated that for every kilogram of prawns caught in the area, about 10 kilograms of other marine life are destroyed. In response to the continuous increases in fishing effort, discussions have started to cap and reform the prawn trawling industry but it remains to be seen whether a truly sustainable solution will be achievable.

Pollution caused by run off from agriculture is another major source of pressure on the Reef. The water quality in inshore areas of the central Great Barrier Reef region is being affected by the discharge of topsoil, nutrients and pesticides eroding from adjacent catchments. This input has increased several-fold since European settlement, with much of the increase occurring in the last 40 years. Many inshore reefs on the central Great Barrier Reef are now dominated by algae rather than corals, and are poor in numbers of species and coral recruits. Coral skeletons indicate that diverse coral communities had prevailed on these reefs in the not too distant past. However, due to a lack of data pre-dating European settlement, the link between the reduced health of inshore reefs and intensified cropping and grazing is still heavily debated.

Global climate change and the rising of ocean temperatures associated with it pose further problems for the Reef. Corals are heat-sensitive – when heat-stressed, they lose the energy-providing microscopic algae that live within them. As a result of prolonged exposure to hot conditions, the normally colourful corals bleach white and die. A mass bleaching event killed large numbers of corals

worldwide in the summer of 1997–98. Ongoing greenhouse gas emissions as well as the projected warming of the tropical waters by an additional 1 to 2 degrees Celsius within the next century give cause for concern that more coral reefs will be damaged in the coming years.

Coral is also vulnerable to damage from the coral-eating crown-of-thorns starfish, a spiny and poisonous species which grows up to 80 centimetres in diameter. Large aggregations of this starfish were first observed on Green Island near Cairns in 1962, where they devoured up to 90 per cent of the corals. The population outbreak moved south along the Great Barrier Reef, and killed large amounts of corals from the reefs in their path. The starfish numbers diminished as their food – the coral – ran out, and eventually the reefs began to recover. In the meantime, however, two more outbreaks have occurred, and it is not clear whether the interval between the outbreaks is long enough for the reefs to recover fully. The causes of the outbreaks remain largely unknown, however, run-off of nutrient-enriched fresh water and overfishing appear to contribute to the build-up of large crown-of-thorns populations.

Within the last few decades, several charismatic species have critically declined in numbers on the Great Barrier Reef. For example, the numbers of breeding loggerhead turtles in Queensland has plummeted in the past twenty years, and the same decline was observed in the number of dugongs over the past 40 years. Hunting, degradation of coastal habitats, off-shore long line fishing, strikes by boat propellers, drowning in trawl nets, disappearing seagrass beds and disturbances of breeding areas all contribute to their decline. The loggerhead turtle is now an endangered species worldwide.

The Great Barrier Reef is an ecological and economic asset to Queensland. Its beauty and richness guarantee an amazing and memorable experience for those who visit it. While it is currently the best-protected large reef system on earth, the World Heritage status is a reminder of our obligation to protect, and thus to use only in a sustainable manner, all parts of the Reef. We need to avoid putting its ecological integrity at risk for the sake of short-term economic profits.

Chapter Editor: Dr Katharina Fabricius

OPPOSITE 'Oxygen', Great Barrier Reef. PHOTOGRAPH: MICHAEL COLLINS

COASTAL DEVELOPMENT

HINCHINBROOK ISLAND, QUEENSLAND

ABOVE Within the forest.
PREVIOUS PAGE Windward side, Hinchinbrook Island.
OPPOSITE Estuary forest.

Hinchinbrook Island is Australia's largest tropical island national park and lies within the Great Barrier Reef World Heritage Area. Protected as a national park since 1932, the island and its shallow channel are biologically rich and environmentally fragile.

Covering 39,000 hectares, Hinchinbrook's vast and diverse beauty has remained largely unspoiled. Rainforest and eucalypt stands grow down to beaches and up to mountainous granite peaks. Its marine habitat areas include fringing reefs, seagrass beds and muddy seabeds that support a wealth of marine life. Hinchinbrook is also home to a high diversity of mangrove forest species.

As well, the island is a significant dugong protection area. These large marine mammals are shy vegetarians, grazing on seagrasses in the island's many shallow and protected waters. More closely related to elephants than to seals or dolphins, the adults grow up to 3 metres in length. Dugongs have few natural predators, but they depend on the maintenance of a pristine marine habitat.

In the Great Barrier Reef region south of Cooktown, their populations have declined to such an extent that they are now classed as critically endangered. Worldwide they are listed as vulnerable to extinction. Most of the indigenous councils of elders that control hunting in the Great Barrier Reef area have suspended dugong hunting south of Cooktown.

The Hinchinbrook Channel and surrounding areas owe their World Heritage listing in part to the fact that they provide a habitat for the dugongs. The shallows around the island harbour a population of approximately 300. These mammals are confined to coastal regions as a result of their dependence on seagrasses, which need the conditions found here to become a nutritious food. Unfortunately, coastal areas are particularly vulnerable to the impact of extreme weather and human activities, such as unwise agricultural practices and residential development, which result in pollution and increased boat traffic. These activities can lead to seagrass loss or contamination, directly harming dugongs or driving them from their feeding grounds. Due to their very slow breeding rate, the decline in their populations is likely to continue if human-induced mortality exceeds 1 to 2 per cent of the females each year.

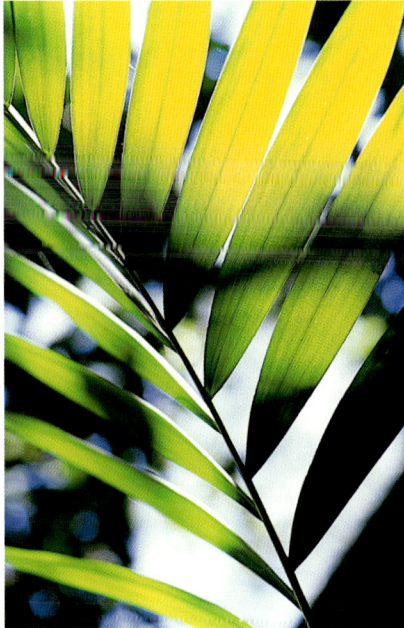

ABOVE Palm frond.
OPPOSITE Hinchinbrook Island.

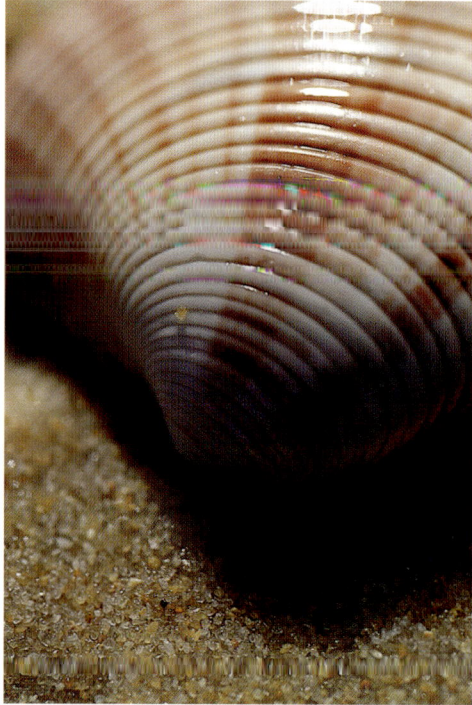

ABOVE An island shell.
OPPOSITE Zoe Bay, Hinchinbrook Island.

LEFT Palm trunk.
OPPOSITE TOP Rainforest vine.
OPPOSITE BOTTOM Mangrove shadow.

The dugongs, as well as other species of marine life, are under serious threat from a planned resort development on the mainland side of the Hinchinbrook Channel. The approved and partially completed development will have a 1500-bed, fully integrated resort and a 210-berth marina complex covering about 140 hectares. The project includes shops, restaurants, a 500-room hotel/motel and about 100 permanent residents. It is estimated that this will double the population of Cardwell, a tourist and fishing town of 1300 people, and will act as a hub for boat traffic in the region.

Development of this area will require the partial clearing of Edmund Kennedy National Park for an airport. Also, the need for new water supplies will mean that dams must be built in the wet tropics area. In addition, developmental practices such as those at Port Hinchinbrook can expose the soil to oxygen, disturbing its chemical balance. Releasing chemicals such as iron sulphide from the soil can lead to the production of large volumes of sulphuric acid and toxic levels of iron and aluminium. The effects on plants, animals, steel concrete structures and human health can be disastrous.

The Senate Inquiry into the Hinchinbrook development found that 'management of the development proposals has been a tragedy of errors' and 'the environment has not been adequately protected' (Hinchinbrook Channel Inquiry, 1999). The development of this resort is inconsistent with conventions on world heritage and biological diversity and a breakdown of our responsibilities towards the Great Barrier Reef World Heritage Area.

Chapter Editor: Professor Frank Talbot

MINING

KAKADU, NORTHERN TERRITORY

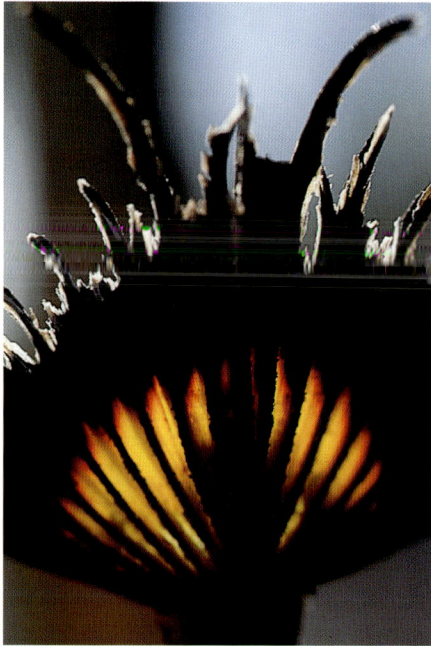

ABOVE Burnt palm.
PREVIOUS PAGE Just before the wet, Kakadu.
OPPOSITE Gorgeous Kakadu.

Kakadu National Park covers 20,000 square kilometres of unspoiled and breathtaking wild lands. It is an area of outstanding biological diversity as well as significant indigenous cultural sites. For these reasons it was declared a national park in 1979 and a World Heritage Area in 1981, with subsequent expansions in 1987 and 1992.

The Mirrar people are the traditional owners of the northern Kakadu area and their management of this region reflects the unique relationship that exists between them and the land itself. Mirrar country includes the Jabiluka mineral lease, the Ranger uranium mine project area, and the mining–tourist town of Jabiru.

For more than twenty years the Mirrar have experienced the negative impact of the massive Ranger uranium mine on their country. In 1996 the Federal Liberal Government lifted bans on new uranium mines imposed by the previous government. The relaxed laws led to several new proposals for uranium mines throughout Australia, including the Jabiluka project inside the

ABOVE Swamp and paperbark forest, Kakadu.
OPPOSITE Burnt shoot.

region of Kakadu National Park. The Mirrar people believe that the development of another mine at Jabiluka will have a continuing negative impact on the Indigenous people in the region and a serious environmental impact on the land. Their words have been quoted: 'What we produce here on earth stays with us.'

Ranger, at Kakadu, is one of the world's largest uranium mines. The ore mined there is finely ground and processed in the mill, where uranium is separated and purified from its carcinogenic radioactive decay products. About 99.7 per cent of the ore becomes tailings – the sludge remaining after grinding and ore treatment. The radioactive nature of the tailings means they must be isolated from the environment for millions of years. Large dams are the most common means of managing tailings, although former open-pit mines are also used.

Ranger will eventually produce 42 million tonnes of tailings and more than 100 million tonnes of waste rock during its operational life. The tailings are being dumped into two mine pits that are not suitable for storage because of the intense tropical rainfall experienced in the region, the high watertable (underground water) and the mine's proximity to floodplains – making contamination inevitable. The radiation hazard from these tailings will be particularly serious.

The design of the Ranger mine underestimated rainfall and overestimated evaporation rates in the region. As a result, massive quantities of contaminated water need to be stored onsite. Pressure on the water-retaining structures has led to over 100 releases of radioactive liquid during the mine's history. The most recent leak at Ranger, in 2000, saw up to 2 million litres of highly contaminated waters leak into Georgetown and Magela creeks. The Jabiluka project areas all lie within the wetlands of Magela Creek, so every leak has the potential to flow quickly into the water and have a detrimental impact on the Kakadu area.

The Mirrar have refused consent for the ore mined at Jabiluka to be transported to Ranger for milling. At an estimated cost of $300 million dollars to build a new mill at Jabiluka, the mine has been on hold since September 1999. This is also due to the continual fall in the price of uranium worldwide. The current facilities at Jabiluka are experiencing the same severe problems with contaminated water management as those encountered at Ranger.

The consequences of uranium mining to the Kakadu area are far-reaching. In tropical regions, the intense monsoonal rains can cause flash flooding and failure of tailings dam structures, causing large-scale pollution of fish and aquatic ecosystems. In the arid region of northern South Australia, the radioactive tailings from the Olympic Dam copper and uranium mine (which will be the largest in the world within a few years) are stored in several tailings dams and will eventually cover an area of up to 12 square kilometres. These dams will reach 10 metres in height – far higher than surrounding sand dunes. The tailings are likely to be inhaled, ingested or absorbed by animals and plants. The radioactive elements in uranium tailings concentrate thousands of times in the food chain, and they are all carcinogenic and mutagenic.

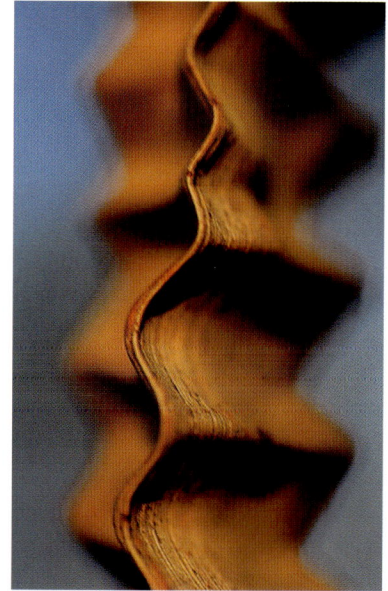

ABOVE Seed pod.
OPPOSITE Burnt pandanas.

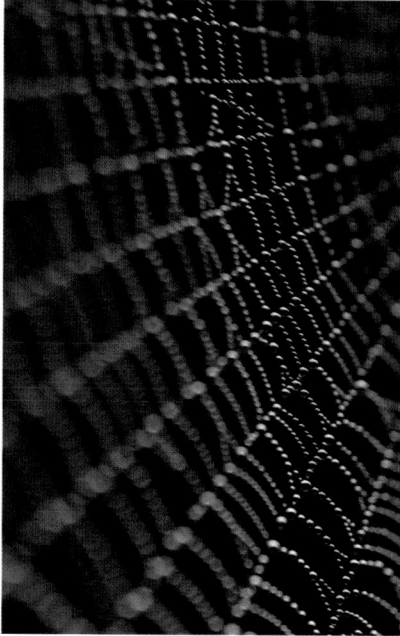

ABOVE Morning dew.
OPPOSITE Before sunrise, burnt forest.

Current Australian regulations call for safeguarding and regulating the tailings for 1000 years, at which time they will still retain some 70 per cent of their original radioactivity. There are approximately 74 million tonnes of uranium tailings presently stored across ten sites in Australia without a satisfactory solution for their long-term management. The radioactive decay of uranium tailings continually produces radon gas – a major cause of lung cancer in uranium miners and nearby environments. Radiation has other effects on human health. If genes in our body cells are altered by radiation, children may be born with an inherited disease or carry a damaged gene transmittable to future generations. Likewise, cancer and leukaemia can be induced when a regulatory gene in an ordinary body cell is damaged by radiation.

A meltdown accident in a nuclear reactor, which can be caused by human or mechanical failure, releases massive quantities of radioactive elements into the atmosphere. The resulting fallout can contaminate soil and food thousands of kilometres away for hundreds of thousands of years. Many European countries are still radioactive after the Chernobyl nuclear power plant exploded in the Ukraine in April 1996. The leftover uranium waste (or spent fuel) from a nuclear reactor is over a million times more radioactive than the original ore, increasing the danger of radiation exposure enormously.

Uranium is not a sustainable source of energy. It strikes no constructive balance between economy, environment and the welfare of people. Renewable energies, on the other hand, including solar, wind, hydro, tidal and biomass, are sustainable and present substantially less risk to current and future generations.

Chapter Editor: Dr Helen Caldicott

NUCLEAR WASTE

THE GREAT VICTORIA DESERT, SOUTH AUSTRALIA

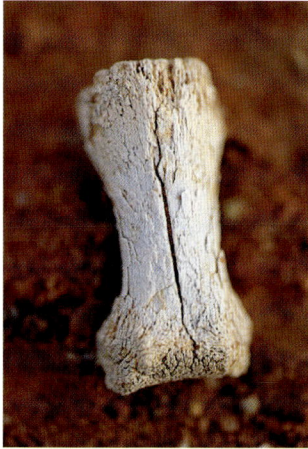

ABOVE 'Desert link'.
PREVIOUS PAGE The Great Victoria
Desert, South Australia.
OPPOSITE Riverbed trees.

The deserts of South Australia are a unique and beautiful landscape that have been formed over millions of years. The current landforms are the result of more than 500 million years of erosion, sedimentation, volcanic activity, long-term global climate change and earthquake activity.

The climactic and geological history of the deserts is shown through many landforms, including the Simpson and Strzelecki dune systems, the great salt lakes of Lake Eyre and the arid rivers which stretch from Queensland to feed it life-giving water, the rocky plains, breakaway country and the unique artesian springs which abound along the southern and western reaches of Lake Eyre. Within this area and into its geological history comes the contemporary story of the Australian Nuclear Waste Facility. This story explains our need and responsibility to house our waste correctly, as opposed to the current plan for waste disposal.

TOP Desert flowers.
ABOVE Lizard skull.
OPPOSITE Lone tree.

The decay of a radioactive element is invisible to human senses, since the various forms of radiation are tasteless, odourless and colourless. The only way to detect radiation is through technology, otherwise it is impossible to know when one has come into contact with radioactive materials. Nature has naturally kept radioactive materials such as uranium to a minimum in surface environments. However, the nuclear age represents a constant threat to the environment because of its potential to increase the amount of radioactivity released to the environment. This happens through leaks, accidents and routine operational releases from uranium mines, nuclear power stations and waste dumps.

These leaks lead to the dispersion of radioactive elements through the ecosystem and food chains. Research has found that exposure to low doses of radiation over a long time can be just as damaging as acute or high-dose exposure in a brief period. This means there is no safe level of radioactive exposure.

Most of Australia's radioactive waste is produced by the ageing research reactor at Lucas Heights in southern Sydney. The reactor was opened on Australia Day in 1958 and is scheduled to be shut down and decommissioned in around 2005, having long passed its effective lifespan. The proposed new reactor, to be built at a cost to taxpayers of just under half a billion dollars, would increase between four- and twelve-fold the amount of radioactive waste generated annually for the next 40 years. An accident at Lucas Heights equivalent to the meltdown at Chernobyl could lead to acute radiation exposure within an 80-kilometre radius; this includes most of Sydney.

All forms of radioactive waste have been produced at Lucas Heights, including large volumes of low-level waste, moderate amounts of both short- and long-lived intermediate waste, and some high-level waste in the form of spent fuel rods. The Australian Government sends most of the spent fuel rods overseas for reprocessing in Europe.

The government plans to dispose of its low-level radioactive waste in the proposed national nuclear dump in the north of South Australia. The safe disposal of existing radioactive waste had been a precondition to the new reactor, yet the government is proceeding with plans to build it without a credible radioactive waste management plan. The people of South Australia have

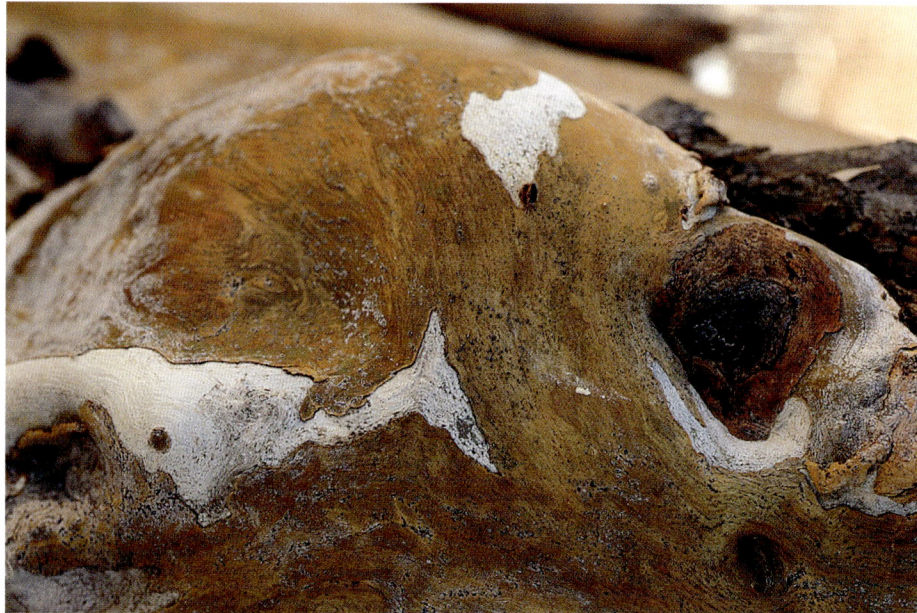

expressed almost unanimous opposition to the proposed low-level waste dump, seeing this as the first step towards accepting the more radioactive intermediate- and high-level waste from Lucas Heights and increasing pressure to open the facility to the global nuclear industry.

This radioactive waste dump, should it be built and begin operating under current plans, will have an engineering integrity of just 300 years and will be operated by either the government or a private company for only 100 years. The waste contained in drums or barrels is to be buried in shallow trenches. After closure of the dump the site would simply be fenced off. Experience from overseas suggests that this type of burial does leak. Therefore these nuclear waste dumps present a high risk of contamination to the surrounding environment and exposed water basin areas.

Despite the virtual absence of surface water there are large reserves of underground water beneath these arid regions of South Australia. The proposed area for the dump lies just south of the Great Artesian Basin and its related aquifers. Most of Lake Eyre is at or below sea level with the southern reaches at 15 metres below sea level. On average, Lake Eyre is thought to flood and fill a few times per century, mainly from heavy rainfalls in the Central Queensland part of the Basin. Smaller parts of Lake Eyre may also partially flood in response to localised rainfall.

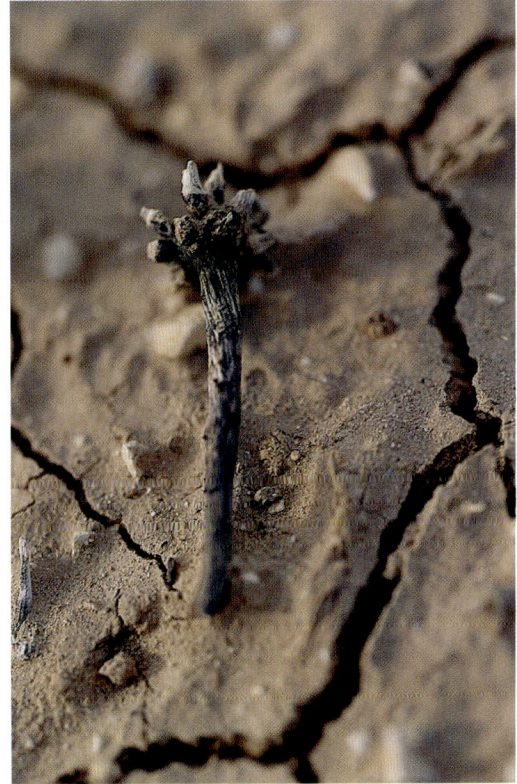

ABOVE Twig face.
OPPOSITE Riverbed tree.

ABOVE Desert branch.
OPPOSITE The desert, South Australia.

The reaction of the desert to a flood is amazing. The usually brown, harsh and salty terrains flourish in green vegetation and wildflowers which paint the landscape in colour, while fish and bird populations explode and breed rapidly, taking full advantage of the unusually abundant water in the lakes. Continued access to unpolluted ground water is essential for most remote communities, as well as for maintaining the flora and fauna and the precious ecosystems of the desert.

Despite billions of dollars being spent on research and the investigation of potential sites over the past five decades, there are no countries that have an approved operational facility for the long-term management and safe disposal of high-level radioactive waste. The solution to managing nuclear waste, as with any hazardous or toxic wastes, is first to make the producers accountable and therefore minimise their production of the waste. Alternative technologies can be used to produce the medical isotopes required by hospitals without the need for nuclear reactors and the burden of the radioactive waste they produce. Secondly, since the transport of the waste is dangerous, the waste needs to be stored on the site of production. The waste must be stored above ground in an accessible dry repository. This was the finding of the Australian Senate Inquiry into the Dangers of Radioactive Waste, which recommended in early 1996 that the 'national waste facility should be engineered for above ground storage', and that it 'be adequately engineered to withstand all possible climatic conditions, no matter how unlikely', to maintain the safety and integrity of all forms of nuclear waste over the time periods required (these being 250,000 years or more).

This approach is more likely to respect and protect the fragile desert ecosystems and the wishes and aspirations of the traditional owners, as well as leading to a more sustainable and equitable society.

Chapter Editor: Dr Gavin M. Mudd

Glossary

Acre a measurement of land area equivalent to 0.405 hectares. (1 acre = 4,4047 m², 1 hectare = 10,000 m²).

Algae a single-cell organism found in surface water ecosystems.

Algal bloom when the nutrient levels in a water body allow algae to grow in massive numbers, choking the water and ecosystem. Algal blooms can be quite toxic to people, cattle and aquatic ecosystems.

Alpha particle a positively charged atomic particle spontaneously emitted by some radioactive substances.

Ammonia common natural and industrial chemical compound consisting of nitrogen and hydrogen (NH_3). Has a strong odour and can be corrosive. Environmentally toxic in high concentrations.

Amphibian an animal that lives on land but breeds in water.

Aquifer a layer of rock or soil that holds water or allows large amounts of water to percolate through it (similar to an underground river).

Barrages weirs constructed in river estuaries to prevent seawater intrusions upstream.

Beta particle an electron or positron spontaneously emitted by some radioactive nuclei. If ingested or inhaled, it can lead to higher biological effects from exposure due to direct contact of the energy with cells.

Billabong a pool of still water formed by a channel or old stream bed leading out from a river.

Biological consisting of living organisms.

Biomass organic matter.

Canopy level the collective covering level of the forest that protects the vegetation beneath.

Carbon dioxide common natural and industrial gas consisting of carbon and oxygen (CO_2). Due to its ability to retain heat, the large amounts of CO_2 being emitted by modern industrial society is causing a build-up of CO_2 in the atmosphere – the principle cause of the Enhanced Greenhouse Effect.

Clear-felling the practice of logging in which virtually all the trees are removed.

Coupe an area of forest which is logged; varying from 10 to 100 hectares.

Critically endangered the last stage before a species of plant or animal becomes extinct in the wild.

E. coli (*Escherichia coli*) a single-celled bacteria that is known for causing many diseases.

Ecosystem a community of organisms interacting with one another and with the environment in which they live.

Endemic native to a particular area and not occurring anywhere else.

Estuary an arm or inlet of the sea; also that part of a river in which its flow meets the sea, and thus where fresh water mixes with salt water.

Fish ladder a constructed system of small pools and gates designed to allow fish to bypass dams and weirs, and travel up and downstream as part of their natural feeding and breeding migrations.

Fission the process of splitting atoms in a nuclear weapon or reactor to release vast amounts of energy. Needs a certain percentage of fissile elements, such as uranium 235 and plutonium-239.

Freehold privately owned land.

Fungi spore-producing plant, for example, mushrooms, moulds, rusts, yeasts etc, that subsists on dead or living organic matter.

Gamma radiation a form of very high energy electromagnetic radiation. Although gamma radiation is physically similar to radio waves, infrared, visible and ultraviolet light, it is not the same due to its high energy and ionising capacity. Gamma radiation can pass through most materials and requires very thick concrete to attenuate its radiative energy.

Geiger counter an instrument for measuring the amount or intensity of radioactivity.

Geology the science which focuses on the composition and changes in the structure of the earth, and the rock formations of which it is comprised.

Giardia gastric bug.

Gondwana (also Gondwanaland) an ancient continent that split to form Africa, South America, Australia, Antarctica, New Zealand and India.

Ground water the water found inside rock formations or soils beneath the earth's surface. Often found in sand, sandstone, limestone and fractured rocks. Most rock formations contain some ground water, although the amount of water (and its ability to move through that rock) will largely depend on the properties of the host rocks.

Habitat the native home of an animal or plant.

Hectare a measurement of land area equivalent to 100 metres by 100 metres, or 2.471 acres.

In-situ leach a mining technique whereby a liquid solution is pumped into the mine to dissolve and transfer the uranium from the ore body into the ground water. This now toxic and radioactive solution is brought to the surface and the uranium is extracted.

Introduced species species of plant or animal not native to a particular area. For example, rabbits and foxes introduced to Australia. These species are native European animals.

Invertebrates animals without a backbone.

Ionising radiation very high energy radiation that can cause chemicals or elements to become charged or ionised. Over time, continued exposure to ionising radiation can lead to a breakdown of materials, such as the containment structures for nuclear waste or cellular materials in biological cells (which leads to increased fatality and disease rates such as cancer in the exposed population).

Iron sulphide a common rock-forming mineral, composed of iron and sulfur (FeS_2). Varieties include pyrite and marcasite.

Isotope any of two or more forms of a chemical element, having the same atomic number, but each having its own particular mass and composition.

Lagoon a shallow coastal lake usually separated from the sea by sand or mud bars.

Lucerne an agricultural crop used for stock feed.

Mangrove tree species that commonly grows on salt, brackish and estuarine mudflats in tidal areas.

Meltdown when nuclear fuel inside a reactor is not cooled sufficiently, the intense heat generated can melt the fuel, which in turn can melt the containment structures at a nuclear power plant and lead to a major environmental catastrophe. The Three Mile Island nuclear accident in the USA in 1979 was a meltdown that was only narrowly averted from breaching the containment structures. The Chernobyl meltdown accident in the former USSR in 1986 led to a massive explosion and dispersed radiation all over Belarus, Europe and Scandinavia.

Microbiological the study of biological species at the micro, or cellular level (less than 1 millimetre in size).

Mine an excavation made in the earth to extract a particular metal or mineral, for example, gold, copper, uranium.

Mutagenic able to induce genetic mutation.

National park an area protected for conservation and recreation purposes by federal or state governments.

Neutron a neutral subatomic particle that is part of all atomic nuclei. When a neutron is captured or crashes into a fissile atom such as uranium-235 or plutonium-239, this causes the atom to split and release vast amounts of energy (fission). Neutrons can pass through virtually any materials.

Nutrient an element that is required for biological growth, such as phosphorus and nitrogen.

Old-growth forest forest that is ecologically mature. Usually has relatively old and large trees and plants, hollows, and shows an absence of disturbance, a low rate of change, and a balance between plant and animal growth and decomposition.

Organic farming farming without the use of artificial chemicals.

Organism any form of animal or plant life.

Plutonium a radioactive metal produced as a by-product of nuclear waste. Can be extracted and used primarily for nuclear weapons, although some countries are now also using it for nuclear power reactors. Not found in nature before the advent of the nuclear industry in the 1940s.

Pulp a moist mass of vegetative fibre used to produce paper.

Pristine retaining its original, intact form.

Radiation the process of releasing energy. The energy released when an atom undergoes radioactive decay is known as ionising radiation, due to its very high energy intensity. The energy can be expressed as gamma waves or beta, neutron or alpha particles.

Radium a naturally occurring radioactive metallic element and also one of the radioactive decay products formed during the breakdown of uranium.

Radon a rare, chemically inert, radioactive gaseous element produced in the disintegration of radium. Radon is an inert gas that decays over time into several intensely radioactive isotopes before decaying into a stable isotope of lead. If inhaled, radon can present a major radiation exposure risk, especially to workers in uranium mines. Radon is considered a major cause of lung cancer in uranium mine workers.

Remnant a small part, quantity or number left remaining.

Repository a place or container where something is stored.

Riparian near the bank of a stream or river.

Saline salty or saltlike; salt dissolved in water or salt left after the evaporation of a lake, etc.

Salinity a concentration of salt.

Sawlog logs large enough for saw milling rather than woodchipping.

Sediment the ground-down particles originally deposited by water, air or ice, that are derived from weathered rock masses. Can be sand, silt or clay.

State forest public forests unprotected from mining and logging.

Supercontinent a large land mass comprised of two or more present-day continents that covered a large part of earth hundreds of millions of years ago.

Systems a combination of things or parts forming a complex or unitary whole, for example, ecosystem.

Tailings the finely ground rock particles left from a mining and milling operation after the element or mineral has been extracted and purified. Often stored in large dams with water, used chemicals and other wastes, tailings can present a substantive environmental risk due to the contaminants they contain. In uranium tailings, for example, about 85 per cent of the original radioactivity remains in the tailings and therefore presents a high risk of radioactive contamination of the environment if they are not adequately stored and isolated for the hundreds of the thousands of years necessary.

Temperate moderate, or cool climate

Uranium a radioactive element, heavy and clay-like in its natural state. Refined and used as a fuel source for nuclear power stations, reactors and weapons.

Urbanisation the spread of cities, towns and industry to rural and natural areas.

Vegetative cover a collection of plants and vegetation over an area. Commonly removed in agriculture and mining.

Veneer thin layer of timber.

Watertable the ground water (aquifer) close to the surface. Often influenced and controlled by rainfall and discharge to surface waters (for example, from rivers and lakes). They provide water to aquatic ecosystems during drought and are therefore critical in maintaining environmental health. Large-scale irrigation and land misuse have led to a significant degradation in watertables, and have created massive salinity problems in many parts of Australia.

Waste Anything left over as excess.

Wilderness large areas of land or waters untouched by technological society – in Australia, they are often maintained and shaped by Aboriginal custodianship.

Woodchips small chips of wood made by putting logs through chipping machines.

World Heritage an area or monument considered to be of international significance that is pinpointed for protection and conservation by the global community as an important part of our natural or cultural heritage.

Chapter Editors

Dr *Helen Caldicott* is a physician, writer, scholar, anti-nuclear campaigner and peace advocate. She has received numerous international awards in recognition of her contribution to international nuclear disarmament, including the Thomas Merton Prize for Peace, 1980, Physicians for Social Responsibility (International Physicians for the Prevention of Nuclear War), Nobel Peace Prize, 1985, and Nuclear Age Peace Foundation, Distinguished Peace Leadership Award, 1994. Dr Caldicott has published several books on disarmament and has been a regular media commentator on the uranium industry in all its forms.

Dr *Katharina Fabricius* is a coral reef ecologist specialising in the influence of the physical environment and human activities on the biodiversity of reefs. She has been involved in research on the Great Barrier Reef and the Red Sea since 1988. Her PhD on reef-inhabiting soft corals was awarded by the University of Munich in 1995.

Mr *Tim Fisher* has co-ordinated many of the Australian Conservation Foundation's land and water ecosystems campaigns over the last ten years, including the Murray–Darling rivers, Snowy River and the Fitzroy Dam campaigns. He is a member of the community advisory committee to the Murray–Darling Basin Ministerial Council, as well as a number of other advisory forums. His own campaign areas cover land and water policy and the ACF's co-operative work with the National Farmers' Federation.

Dr *Pierre Horwitz* currently works as the Director of the Consortium for Ecosystem Health at Edith Cowan University in Perth, Western Australia. Dr Horwitz has completed numerous research programs and consultancies for government, industry and community groups. His research experience covers aquatic fauna, the health of inland aquatic ecosystems and environmental management. Dr Horwitz has a particular interest in the history of land and water use in Australia, the relationship between human health and the health of the surrounding ecosystems.

Professor *Jamie Kirkpatrick* is Professor of Geography and Environmental Studies at the University of Tasmania, where he teaches courses in vegetation management and natural environment field techniques, and undertakes research in the area of conservation ecology. He won the POL Eureka Prize for environmental research in 1997 for his work on the conservation of plant communities and species.

Kakadu after burn.

Dr Gavin M. Mudd is Research Fellow in Mine Waste Hydrology in the Department of Civil Engineering, University of Queensland. The areas of expertise Dr Mudd has developed include hydrology, ground water, geochemistry and computer modelling. His particular interests include the environmental impact and management of mining, mine waste disposal, especially uranium mining, radioactive wastes and the impact of acid mine drainage. Some of his major research to date includes the impact of in-situ leach ('solution') uranium mining, the environmental impact and rehabilitation of abandoned uranium mines, plus current problems at operational mines.

Dr Hugh Spencer is Director of Research at the Cape Tribulation Tropical Research Station operated by the AUSTROP Foundation, of which he is a founding director. A conservation biologist based in Far North Queensland, he is an active conservationist and is deeply involved in efforts to save the lowland Daintree tropical forests, which are under increasing pressure through settlement. He has lived in the area for over thirteen years.

Professor Frank Talbot is currently Adjunct Professor, Graduate School of the Environment, Macquarie University, and Director Emeritus, US National Museum of Natural History, Smithsonian Institution. Professor Talbot's career has centred on research into the ecology of coral reef fishes in Tanzania, New Guinea, Australia and the US Virgin Islands, and research into estuarine fishes and on tuna in South Africa. He has served as president of the Marine Sciences Association of Australia and the Great Barrier Reef committee. He has published some 60 scientific publications and collaborated on five books on marine biology.

Dr Barry Traill is a zoologist who has worked on the ecology and conservation of temperate forests and woodlands for twenty years, since his boyhood in Gippsland. His area of expertise is the effects of logging on wildlife. He has worked with state wildlife departments, conservation organisations and industry on ecology and conservation issues.

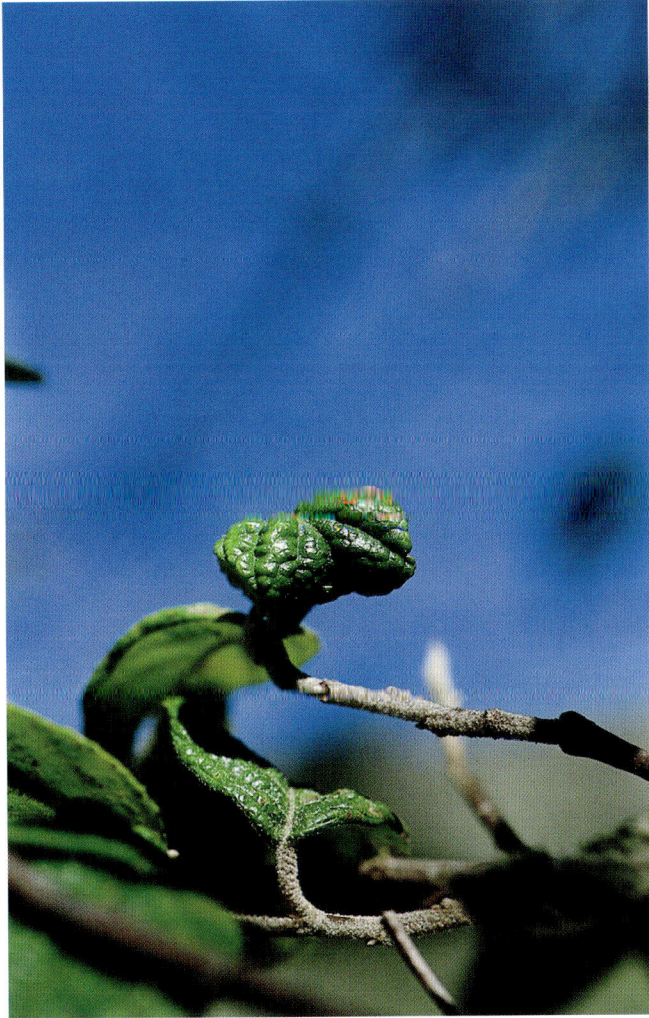

—